I trust everyth
practitioner wh̲ ̲ ̲ ̲ ̲ ̲ ̲
someone shaping kingdom leaders in the classrooms of academia. Soak in these words!

Alan Briggs
Leadership Coach, Author
Lead Creative at Stay Forth Designs

By definition, the apostolic journey is antithetical to the walking of groomed pathways. In *Through Barren Wastelands*, Benesh dares us to consider how we might cut fresh trails into urban centers for the cause of Christ. We are reminded that the old models aren't worth the time, and that pioneering—a much harder standard—is well worth the effort.

Josh Feit
Creative Director, Encompass World Partners

Sean, through his unique style of raw and personal storytelling, takes us deeper into the world of frontier leadership. While often overlooked and undervalued, Sean gives us both a lens and a language to recognize what these leaders look like, and why they are so vital to the future of the church.

Tim Catchim
Planter, Coach, Consultant, and Co-author of *The Permanent Revolution: Apostolic Imagination and Practice for the 21st Century Church*

What I get the most out of Sean Benesh's books, especially *Through Barren Wastelands*, is the nontypical and outside-the-box writing that you do not get when you read just about any book on church planting. In *Through Barren Wastelands*, you are not going to be thrust headlong into forms and models of church planting. Instead, it is more like going on an adventure to somewhere you have never heard of, much less visited. They are not the typical suburban white neighborhoods that church planters are flocking to. They may be low-income, unsightly, geographically isolated, and small. All the things that work against a church planter who wants to be in "full-time" ministry. But for those who desire to share the gospel and seek the welfare of a community, these are beautiful places, filled with people that need Jesus. Sean helps the reader to see a biblical means of truly loving our neighbor. By establishing startups and non-profits in these places, there is the opportunity to offer new life to these hard-hit communities. Along the way in this adventure, you learn something about yourself. To find out if you are an explorer, pioneer, or a misfit, you will just have to read the book. You will not be disappointed.

Wesley T. Satterfield
Coffee Roaster and Misfit

This book may not be pleasant to read, there is an honest appraisal of North American church planting that we may not like to hear. Yet, the thoughts contained are necessary. Dr. Benesh challenges us. I spent a good portion of my life in church planting amongst least-reached peoples (Muslim and Buddhists). What I need now is a good kick in the pants to get beyond "normal" and settling. This has been a welcome, and for me personally, soul-inspiring push to go beyond the norm and live a life of risk and adventure for the sake of the gospel.

Ted Offutt
Director of Training, Encompass World Partners

THROUGH BARREN WASTELANDS

SEAN BENESH

Through Barren Wastelands: In Search of Explorers, Pioneers, Misfits, and the Apostolic Imagination

Published by Intrepid. www.intrepidmissions.com

The mission of Intrepid is to elevate marginalized communities and people through training church planters, pastors, and missionaries to start social enterprises to sustain themselves long-term so they can seek the betterment of these overlooked and neglected places and people as they start new churches, businesses, and non-profits.

Intrepid
2034 NE 40th Ave. #414
Portland, OR 97212

Manufactured in the United States of America.

ISBN: 978-0-578-23639-1

Contents

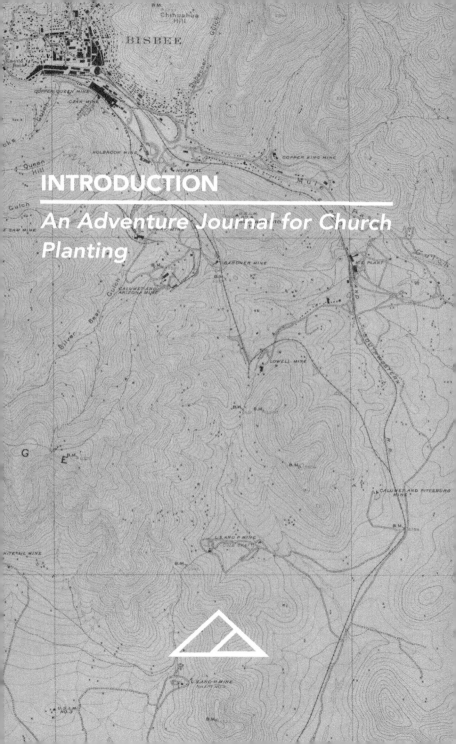

INTRODUCTION

An Adventure Journal for Church Planting

For some odd reason I've entered a season of life where both my paid ministry and professional worlds have collided. Well, maybe not so much collided as aligned. In leading Intrepid I constantly wade into the waters of calling, identity, vocation, and bivocational ministry. Conversely, in the classroom I've been teaching a particular course related to vocation, identity, and purpose.

This is not simply a one-off course, but I teach it both in a traditional undergrad setting as well as an accelerated adult learning format.

What that means is I teach it six-to-seven times a year. These kinds of conversations are constantly at the forefront of my thinking. As a result, and based upon my previous book *The Adventure of Vocation*, I see this whole topic of vocation as an adventure and a journey.

In our own adventure or journey in life we continue to learn more about who we are and how to be more comfortable in our own skins. The way life is, I know things now about myself that I desperately wish I had known in my 20s and 30s. One a-ha moment was the realization that I need to keep a sense of wanderlust or adventure constantly before me. If I don't, I feel like I'll simply shrivel up and disappear.

While that may sound like a recipe for jet-setting around the globe, I'm not talking about that. Instead it's this sense of where I'm allowing my imagination to wander as well as to pursue curiosities and interests. What that looks like on a weekly basis is to spend time reading books on historical adventures, current explorations, and travels as well as exploring my own city and region with my sons. I've found it's enough to satiate these desires and leanings. I also realized that in my own writings I've steered away from my own kind of adventure writings ... until now.

No, this is not a journal where I recount summiting a remote peak in Alaska nor about losing myself in slot canyons in northern Arizona. Instead, it's about an adventure of a different sort. One that is tied to vocation, identity, and living on the frontier of God's mission to the world. I love all of the adventures and travels I've been on; they were definitely fun and I want more. However, they cannot and could never replace the thrill of adventure living out the calling I sensed God placed on my life when I surrendered all at the age of eighteen.

What you have in your hands is an attempt to recapture God's mission to the world as an adventurer who gets word of a far-off remote mountain range that has never been mapped. It is time to take the plunge and head out. Our journey awaits.

Through Barren Wastelands

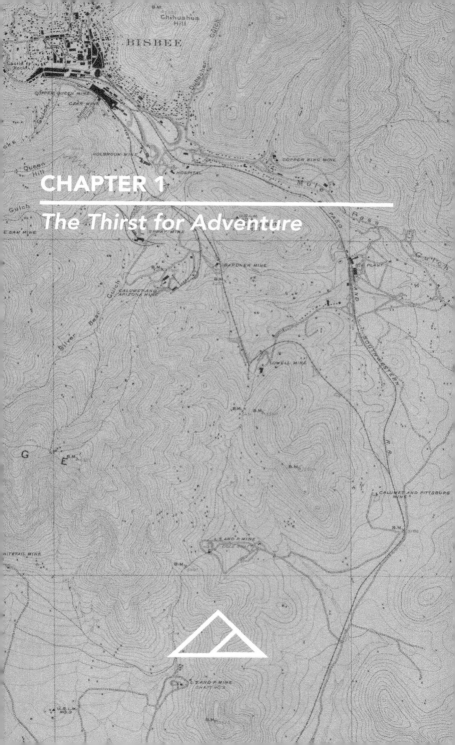

CHAPTER 1
The Thirst for Adventure

I get restless. Always have. And I mean *always*. The "where" of what I was drawn to at the moment has changed over the years. But the common denominator still remains the same ... exploring what *to me* is the frontier. As you can imagine, if the frontier represents the leading edge of my experiences then it certainly is evolving and moving.

It was this restlessness, and a sense of calling that compelled me to lead my family to the Pacific Northwest now over ten years ago. In that regard the frontier was not wilderness, but urban. An immigrant and refugee neighborhood in Vancouver, British Columbia, to be exact. It was every bit as new to me as exploring the deep canyon lands in northern Arizona.

When we first moved to Portland, the newness of the adventure satiated some of my restlessness. I had a new city to explore and learn about. There were and are many layers and wrinkles to uncover in this ever-changing complex city. In that regard, it still continues to be a new frontier to explore even after years. However, every now and then I just need to leave the city and explore the hinterlands.

For the first several years those trips always meant making a beeline straight for the coast. Maybe since I grew up in Iowa and lived in the Arizona desert for nearly a decade it made sense why the Pacific Ocean beckoned me. We'd explore the small coastal towns and craggy coastline during every trip. Sitting on a high cliff watching the rhythm of the waves pounding the coast is as good as it gets.

But I wanted more.

I became restless with my journeys. So I headed east. East of Portland that is. Crossing to the other side of the Cascade Mountains is to step into a completely different world. Different than urban Portland and certainly different than the rain-drenched Oregon coast. From rainforest to high desert in the matter of an hour's drive. From a color palette of dark greens, grays, and blues to one filled with browns sprinkled in with a touch of green. It didn't matter what color it was. I needed it.

This restlessness, left unchecked, results in a build-up of pressure. Pressure isn't all bad. After all, it was the pressure of magma that created the majestic Cascade Mountains and the line of volcanic peaks that run down the spine of Oregon. The peaks that were created under pressure now became the ones to alleviate my pressure within. And so a road trip was in store.

I had it all mapped and planned out. A camping trip atop a central Oregon desert mountain. Even though it was summer, it was high enough in elevation that the evenings were cool and crisp. On Friday morning (today is the Sunday two days removed) we loaded up our SUV and began our journey up and over the Cascades. From Portland it is a steady climb up as the road takes us up the flank of Mt. Hood. While starting at nearly sea level in Portland, the highway peaks at 4,000 feet in the town of Government Camp before beginning the descent down the backside.

The drive up weaves its way through dark and brooding forests. The large trees so hem in the road that one is rarely afforded any views other than the channel that the road cuts through the trees. As the road winds up higher and closer to Government Camp, sure enough there are breaks in the view and on a clear day the glaciated peak of Mt Hood stares down at us. I've seen this view countless times. It never gets old, and yet I wanted something new. And so we kept driving.

The funny thing about "new" is that there is no universally agreed-upon definition of the word or how we judge something to be new. I grew up in small-town Iowa. I couldn't wait to leave, get out, and explore. Living in a place like the Pacific Northwest, Oregon, Portland, and the inner NE neighborhood of the Hollywood District is new for me. But I know many people who grew up here, who, like I was in Iowa, can't wait to leave, get out, and explore. What's new for me may not be new for you.

The high desert of central and eastern Oregon beckons me. I have spent a good bit of time lately reflecting on why. Why not the spectacular Oregon coast? Why not the lush rainforests on the western slopes of the Cascade Mountains? Why not all of the oddities of Portland? Why the barren desert?

Still to this day no other landscape has captured my imagination like the desert. For most people, a desert is kind of "nothing to see here." During my stint as a hiking and mountain biking guide in Southern Arizona, I learned that we actually have four primary deserts in the United States: Chihuahuan, Sonoran, Mojave, and the Great Basin. Even though they are all deserts, they are distinct from one another in flora and fauna, annual rainfall, elevation, and more.

While living in Tucson we'd sometimes drive east to Las Cruces, New Mexico, and I'd try to point out and identify the transition between the Sonoran and Chihuahuan deserts. I'd look for the telltale signs of vegetation. Sure enough, we'd transition from the land of the picturesque saguaro cactus into a new land of desert sage.

But my love for deserts was about more than their unique characteristics. It was also about the human story.

Being a hiking and mountain biking guide afforded me innumerable hours in the desert poking around, peeking under mesquite trees, circumnavigating around stately saguaros, avoiding prickly pear, brushing up against soap tree yuccas, and learning to spot Hohokam pottery from a distance.

Contemporaries of the more well-known Anasazi, the Hohokam also disappeared midway through the fifteenth century. We still don't know what "disappeared" means other than that their way of life ceased. Many historians surmise they simply migrated or became part of modern-day tribes like the Tohono O'Odham that are still in southern Arizona. Either way, it may have been timely since the first European to come through the area was the Franciscan friar Marcos de Niza in 1539.

During many hikes, mountain bike trips, and explorations into the desert, I learned to be pretty adept at finding pottery shards left by the Hohokam. While you can easily find them at the Catalina State Park or in a museum, walk down nearly any wide wash and along the banks, and, if knowing what to look for, you'll always find pieces. Some have abrupt edges as if they had recently been broken while other pieces have been worn down from having been sent on a tumble down the wash during a flash flood.

Holding these pieces in my hand or following the lines of village walls or foundation stones from pit houses created a hunger in me to know more. Who were these people? Why did they choose to live *here?* Why were their villages arrayed in a certain way? Why didn't they grow and become larger cities like in Chaco Canyon in New Mexico, Cahokia east of St. Louis or even Teotihuacan in central Mexico? So I did what any other curiosity-driven person would do. I read. I explored. And I read some more.

What I didn't realize was this would become a major turning point in my life. While there are both major and minor narratives in this storyline, in terms of the trajectory of this chapter, what really comes to mind is this: I became fascinated with ancient urban developments in addition to modern-day cities. I had made the full transition. From one who grew up in rural America and who hated cities to one who had grown to love and embrace cities and couldn't wait to find out and explore more of them.

I was already a church planter. Forgot to mention that detail. If you've read any of my previous books, then you might recall other stories of me, working as a hiking and mountain biking guide. In the context of church planting I worked as a guide because I was (and still am) horrible at raising funds. I can't and won't stand before crowds or leadership teams to fabricate details about cities or people I'm trying to connect with simply to garner sympathy and money. It's not in me. If you want in, let's do this; if not, I'll just work and make it happen. That's why I was a guide.

I realized that the same reason I loved being a guide and a church planter was that ultimately both were rooted in the same impulse ... a craving for adventure. Mind you, I don't mean this in some mind-numbing narcissistic way. Instead, it was into this context of exploring and stepping into a life of adventure and missions that I had surrendered my life once I came to faith in Christ. I believe that God in his graciousness and omniscience knew so intimately who I was that when I sensed he called me into this direction, it was a no-brainer. Sign me up.

Ironically though, I've already had a lifetime of adventure and explorations and have never lived outside of North America. One would think this would compel me to travel all over the world on countless and endless adventures. But I didn't. I have enough here. In that regard I find a kindred spirit in Edward Abbey who notes in *Desert Solitaire* that one could spend a lifetime in Arches National Park, where he wrote the book, and still never uncover all of its nooks and crannies. I felt the same way in Arizona and I certainly feel the same way in the Pacific Northwest.

It's hard for me to think of gallivanting all over the world if I haven't even explored one percent of the place I call home. That's where this hunger and thirst for adventure is not and can never be satiated. However, this is also where there is a bit of an obstacle in the way. Maybe call it a fork in the road ... or better yet on the trail. An abrupt fork that comes out of nowhere. This is where my personal sense of adventure and exploration diverges from that of church planting.

Recently in a conversation a question was thrown out ... are church planters explorers, pioneers, or settlers? Easy. Settlers. No hesitation. Church planting in North America has lost its pioneer or explorer ethos. Instead, it's a great career move and an opportunity to relocate to a city and neighborhood where you've always wanted to live. Portland is now a city full of church-planting settlers. The pioneers and explorers have since moved on or are looking elsewhere.

To be fair. There's a canyon-like gap in how a similar question is asked today versus 200 years ago. Around that time Lewis and Clark floated by what is now the edge of Portland seeking a watery route to the Pacific Ocean. Between here and St. Louis it was nothing but expansive and relatively unknown wilderness ... apart from what the fur trappers and mountain men knew. And of course, since history tends to be written by the victors, this also fails to consider that there were roughly 100 million inhabitants in the Americas when the first European showed up.

While I may think of a place like Portland great for settlers in regards to church planting, each one might as well be Lewis and Clark. Whether having grown up in the pastoral Midwest, the humid South or the coastal Southeast, a move to Portland would be for them as exotic as moving half-way around the world to Mumbai.

It would be arrogant on my part to assume I'm a pioneer or explorer in the truest sense. I live in a land long ago explored and mapped. Settled. While Portland certainly had a colorful past, today it is the home of tech workers, graphic designers, startup entrepreneurs, and a whole lot of people who'd be deemed as normal. But then isn't this notion of exploring or pioneering truly about one's own perspective?

I can imagine Lewis and Clark on their expedition floating down the massive Columbia River. Near the point it dumps into the Pacific Ocean it is terrifyingly wide. For them this was an era of discovery. For all of the tribes they encountered, whether on the plains, in the Rockies, or along the Columbia, this was not a blank spot on *their* map. They knew it. It is the same dynamic for church planters moving to places like Portland. But it isn't exclusive to church planters. People who immigrate to Portland from other nations also go through this experience.

In the most recent college class I taught, I had a student from Guam. She was the first in her large family to leave the island and come to the mainland. There were for her tears and waves of culture shock and adjustment. What was new for her, again, was home for many already here. While she represented the explorer and pioneer in her family, most everyone else now in Portland are settlers. This is the push-and-pull dynamic of cities. It happens to you. It happens to me.

So what is this thirst for adventure? Are there geographic boundaries or parameters to it? Is there an end to it? Do explorers become pioneers and then eventually settlers? That seems to be the route for church planting. From pioneer missionary to teaching pastor of a church. I've had many conversations with people who love planting, who once the gatherings start find themselves inexplicably sliding into a more pastoral role. Some notice it and hate it. For others it is a welcome transition. Does that mean it is time to move on again?

By the time I rolled into this summer I was coasting on fumes. My tank was depleted. I was spent. It was an intense and overwhelming academic year. Towards the end I had to do everything in my power to keep from pulling the eject lever. But I made it. I got to summer. If there was a way, I'm not sure how, I've somehow been able to place the academic side of me into hibernation. Cryo-sleep. Dormant.

But I needed to feed and nurture my soul. So I began binge-reading books on nature, the outdoors, explorers, and the like. I read a couple books by Edward Abbey, books about conquistadors in South America, the flight and plight of Geronimo and the Chiricahua Apache, Aldo Leopold, the journey of Everett Ruess, and more. While these works certainly fed my soul and fueled my imagination, it did much more than that. It gave me new ways to look at the state of church planting here in the U.S.

Through Barren Wastelands

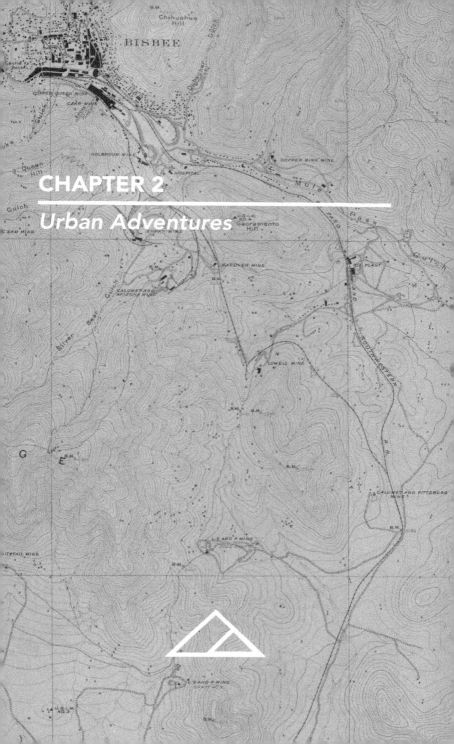

CHAPTER 2
Urban Adventures

When we talk of adventures, we conjure up images of ascending distant and inaccessible peaks, exploring nameless canyons in the American Southwest, or plummeting over precipitous waterfalls on a whitewater rafting trip. I've done those. Loved them. Look forward to doing more. But since when does adventure have geographic boundaries? Even more so, why do we assume adventures happen "over there" and never "here?"

It was an abrupt transition for me. Never in my wildest dreams could I have imagined it.

For a long stretch, I stopped exploring the hinterlands. The wild. The rural. The wilderness. The blank spaces on my personal map. Instead my attention, fascination, and heart turned towards the city. Mind you, this was in a smallish desert city of a million people. But something changed within. Something clicked. It was as if a whole new world began opening up before me. An enormous swath of blank spaces on the map I had never seen before nor realized.

The city.

As I've been poring over Edward Abbey's non-fiction writings this summer, there's most certainly a theme that comes up repeatedly. His utter disdain for cities (and even technology). It's probably no surprise that he'd prefer living alone in the nude in the bowels of the Grand Canyon than spend an hour in the city. That's probably a sentiment shared by many. As a result, in any talk of adventure, exploration, and new vistas never are cities involved.

But the city became my frontier.

The metamorphosis for me was almost instantaneous. One minute I was knocking around the desert with my family camping in the high alpine meadows, exploring ancient ruins, and jumping into perennially-flowing desert streams. The next minute I was walking around downtown Tucson, reading voraciously about my city and cities in general, taking my family to all kinds of city adventures ... parades, restaurants, cafes, historic sites, new developments, and more. It was so new and intoxicating that I completely severed ties with the wilderness ... at least the one that lies outside the city.

It wasn't intentional. It just happened. Like being swept downstream by a ferocious river after your boat capsizes, I was pulled into the heart of the city. I didn't resist. Didn't want to. I pointed my feet downstream and let the current take me. It most certainly did.

It was over ten years later that I discovered I still had my hiking boots from all of those previous years of outings, hikes, and explorations. They sat dormant in the bottom of my closet. Hidden away. It was as abrupt of a change that anyone could make. That trajectory then sent us to move into a high-density neighborhood full of immigrants and refugees in Vancouver, British Columba and again to move into the heart of Portland. I was all-in. The metamorphosis was complete.

After they lay suffocating in my closet for over a decade, I pulled my boots out one day. Since we do still go and explore the hinterlands on occasion—a reconnection—I wanted my boots for a hike to a waterfall in the Columbia Gorge. At the trailhead I laced them up. Still comfortable and fit around my feet as if I had only had them off yesterday rather than a decade ago. It was like meeting an old friend and picking up the same conversation after a decade of not seeing each other.

Either it was me or my boots, but somehow I got the news. It was simply not the same. Time and distance had eroded our relationship. Not only that, but they worn away the glue in the sole of my boots. Half-way through an easy stroll they gave out. The sole exploded and fell apart. I hobbled back to the trailhead. I guess the boots couldn't take the years of neglect and solitude. They knew something was up. Something had changed.

My reading diet changed. From reading about ancient Hohokam to gentrification and the rise of the Creative Class in cities. I've now read (and written) countless books and articles on urban planning, transportation planning, the built environment, understanding cities, and the like as they relate to ministry and particular church planting. Edward Abbey would not be pleased. From fellow desert sojourner to now me a citified guy. I'm sure he'd have choice words for me and not hold anything back.

Admittedly my summer reading schedule has been mostly an abrupt break from all-things academia and books on the city. Since I coasted into this summer on fumes I needed to take a mental break, which is why I spent a good chunk of time exploring the Southwest desert in the writings of Abbey. I too needed a reprieve from life in the city. Although mostly mental, I've journeyed far and wide with Abbey ... exploring slot canyons, rafting down the Colorado River, hiking above the timberline at 11,000 feet to escape the summer heat, and reflecting on the ferocity of desert life. He drew my heart and imagination deeper into adventure.

But we never think of cities as the repository of adventure. Back in Arizona, I'd regularly snatch up my family and take them on excursions deep into the desert or high up in the mountainous sky islands. Now? Most of our excursions are in the city or smaller communities within a quick jaunt from Portland. We walk, explore, observe, take photos, eat food, and drink coffee. That's it. That's the equation. Simple math.

Yesterday was one such outing. A ten-minute drive and we were transported into a different world called South Waterfront. Sitting across the imaginative southern boundary of downtown Portland is this high-rise development. It's new, sleek, modern. The first time we saw it after moving from Vancouver we all shouted in unison, "It looks like Vancouver!" It most certainly does.

The plan was simple. Drive there, park, and explore. With cameras in hand we set out to do just that. And we did. We wandered up and down streets, stepped into green spaces, and took hundreds of photos. It produced the same emotions and euphoria as when we used to (and still do) explore the wilderness areas. The only difference is that this is the city.

But that's where the differences end. Mind you, those are pretty substantial differences. Same emotions, though. Instead of wondering what's around the next bend in the trail or the next vista that overlooks the expansive desert, we're anticipating what's around the corner of the next building, hoping for an interesting alley (not in South Waterfront), and interesting pedestrian traffic.

We'd walk. We'd stop. Contort our bodies to take all kind of photos. Breathe. Take in the sights and sounds. Eventually we wound our way to the aerial tram which takes you up the West Hills to the top where OHSU (Oregon Health and Science University) is perched high up. The ride up was sublime and scenic. We talked. Took photos. Soaked in the views of the city we love and have called home for the past nine years.

As we reached the top we continued to walk around, take more photos, laugh, and stand as the panoramic views of Portland spread out below us. As impressive as the Grand Canyon? No, nothing is. But this is a view and a place of adventure that has yet to satiate our appetites.

I wonder if church planting is still the adventure that lured me in almost twenty years ago. If I know me (and I think I do ... sort of) I know I'm drawn inexplicably to new experiences, adventures, and the pull towards creating from scratch. In the ministry world that is the perfect recipe for church planting. Or was.

If church planting was for explorers or pioneers, what I see today is a landscape filled with settlers. Portland, billed by many as one of the last frontiers of North American missions, is certainly far from that. Never really was that. Now? The density of church planting, churches, and ministries has me more convinced than ever that it's a land settled. It doesn't mean there's not work to be done. But for the explorers and pioneers? Well, they're already straining their necks for the next vista.

I know I am.

So what does any of this mean? It seems as though for the past decade, denominations, ministries, and church planting networks went all-in on cities. Unfortunately, this trend also runs on parallel tracks with gentrification. Meaning, in the mid-twentieth century, during White Flight, as white people left the city for the suburbs, there was an uptick in new church plants on the city periphery and city churches relocating to the suburbs. Fast forward the storyline and it is eerily similar. As white people have flooded back into working class and minority urban neighborhoods, there's been a massive shift to church planting in these gentrifying neighborhoods.

Unfortunately, one of the unintended consequences is that, as new research shows, white church plants in the city actually assist in propelling gentrification and the resultant displacement of minorities. It's as if we need a book like *When Helping Hurts* for church planting in the city.

The tension before me is this ... how do we conceive of or frame church planting on the ever-moving frontier of missions that doesn't damage communities? To truly be a blessing and an asset. To do so in a posture of humility and servanthood rather than in a colonial expansionist mindset. Maybe it's time to also change our language. No more "penetrating lostness" or "expanding the Kingdom" or "pushing back darkness" and so on. Instead, we need to emulate Jesus who came to serve and give his life away. That always resonates.

This is the tension I seek to reconcile in my own heart and mind as an educated white male. How do we reclaim the ethos, mindset, and lifestyle of pioneer or frontier missions without the damaging consequences of colonialism?

In my summer reading binge of adventure books, I'm currently working through *Majestic Journey: Coronado's Inland Empire* by Stewart Udall. The book follows the conquistador Francisco Vasquez de Coronado as he led a regiment of troops from Mexico City up through Mexico, into Arizona, through New Mexico, and ultimately into Kansas. Since we get the bulk of our American history from the British perspective and life after Plymouth Rock, which was founded in 1620, we forget that the Spanish were already trekking all over the United States before that.

In 1527, Álvar Núñez Cabeza de Vaca travelled from Florida all of the way across the continent, through the Southwest and eventually all of the way to Mexico City. Then there was the North African Moor Esteban and the French Fray Marco who pushed into Arizona in 1539 (Esteban had previously traveled with de Vaca). Some even contend that the first non-native in Arizona was not a European, but an African, Esteban himself. Then in 1540, Coronado began his expedition returning in 1542. In the same year Juan Rodriguez Cabrillo sailed up the west coast as far as Oregon.

There is no denying that life after Contact (1492) wrecked havoc on life in North America. Over ninety percent of the indigenous population were either slaughtered or died from the diseases introduced by these Europeans. As I mentioned earlier, there's now data that shows new white church plants in gentrifying neighborhoods are actually doing more harm than good. This is fresh off research conducted for a PhD dissertation at Portland State University by my friend Dave Kresta. As I read his findings, I couldn't help by think of the parallels between colonialist expansion in the Americas and this present-day phenomenon.

Now, am I saying that modern-day white church planters are operating in the same mindset as sixteenth-century Spanish conquistadors? Absolutely not. What I *am* saying is that the effort to explore (or conquer) new frontiers has devastated local indigenous populations. In the case of church planting today, it is abetting the gentrification process.

How do we engage in church planting and pioneer missions without causing more damage than good? How do we that in urban areas and rural alike?

Through Barren Wastelands

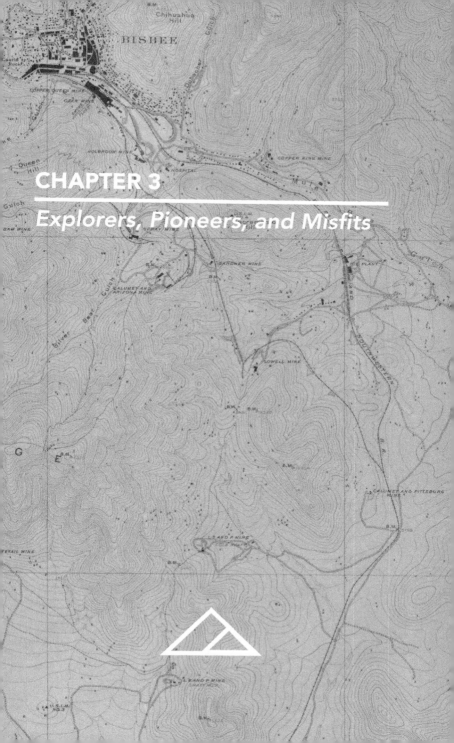

CHAPTER 3

Explorers, Pioneers, and Misfits

I was not prepared for any deep work of the soul this past summer. I simply wanted a reprieve. A mental vacation. To break free, cut loose, and let my mind wander. That's why I devoured book after book. While it wasn't apparent to me when I started, looking back I saw a clear pattern emerge.

I was hungering for adventure.

That would seem like a recipe for traveling widely, exploring new wrinkles in the landscape, and making memories. My son's second surgery left us mostly homebound apart from regular excursions into the urban wilderness to walk, take photos, explore, talk, and drink coffee.

My books not only took me on new adventures, but began casting off some of the shackles that were holding me back from living the life God wired me for. Yesterday I finished reading about the adventures of Coronado in the early sixteenth century that I mentioned in the previous chapter. As soon as I put that book down, I picked up another on the life and history of the Anasazi who lived in the American Southwest. In each and every book I've read this summer there was one common thread throughout ... stories of grand expeditions, adventure, travel, and new frontiers.

All throughout the hours spent each week with my nose in a book sitting out on our fourth story balcony above a noisy intersection with a mix of pedestrians, people on bikes and in cars, I would be swept away to far-off places. Not as an escape ... or maybe it was. Each story also took me back to familiar places I once knew in the sense of a forgotten mindset, vocation, and calling. None of which have ever left me, but which to some extent had gone into hibernation.

It was a hunger and thirst for new adventures and frontiers that had compelled us to move to the Pacific Northwest. However, after ten years here I realized I had become too complacent. I didn't (or don't) dream as much. I stopped daydreaming. Under the constant pressure to provide, and establish and advance a career, I suppressed the deep work of God in my heart. Not that God doesn't want me to provide for my family, work hard, and so on, but I began living other people's lives. Like the hypocrites of old, I was wearing the masks of others. Acting. Not being who God made me to be.

I should've known better. Besides, I teach on this. Every fall I teach what is called a First Year Learning Community (FYLC) at Warner Pacific University. It's more than an academic class. It's a combination of a church-small-group meets support-group meets academic class. The idea came about as a result of having so many first-generation college students. The FYLC was designed to help students adjust and find help navigating their first year in school.

Early on in the semester, we talk a lot about understanding who we are. We tell stories. We share our personal stories. Our past. Our family. Our upbringing. At times these are intense and emotional.

The thing about our stories, especially early on, is none of us have any control over them. We didn't choose where we were born. We didn't choose our parents. Our genetics. Our ethnicity. Our personality. Our gifts. What we discover is how all of this made us into who we are today, and then of equal importance, what we're going to choose to do with it.

I didn't choose to be curious. A wanderlust at heart. Longing deeply for the frontier ... wherever and whatever that may be. When I look back on my adult life, the moments and years I felt most alive were when I was in a place doing precisely what God wired me for. When I came to faith in Christ right out of high school, I felt simultaneously compelled to give my life away as a missionary. I had no idea what that even meant. But now more and more I see what that means.

Whenever and wherever I have lived on what was for me the leading edge of mission, my life was filled with meaning, purpose, and passion. Money and career were purely secondary in the sense that they were not the goals I was pursuing. It was and is a calling that has so riveted me that anytime I attempt to deviate from its course I'm left deflated and almost numb. Does that make me an adventure junkie? While it might sound like it, that is farthest from the truth, especially for those who know me.

The point is that God wired me to be a pioneer ... an explorer ... a misfit that unless what I'm doing is aimed in that direction, I'm miserable.

There have been two instances when I attempted to move away from this calling and wiring to pursue sensible career choices. One was a denominational job where I was office-bound apart from trips to meet with church planters in the state. Within weeks I was already recognizing that my soul was shriveling. I began to escape the office as much as I could. I'd rent a car, drive an hour and a half just to meet with a church planter for coffee.

The second experience was conducting academic research at a state university. I had my little cubicle overlooking the urban plaza below. Each day I'd sit in my coffin (cubicle) at the computer withering away. I was trapped and surrounded by a world I couldn't wait to escape from. I had previously thought being a stuffy academic was in the cards for me. But then I had an encounter with the true me and I took the mask off.

These experiences were formative. It's not that they were bad or wrong or anything like that. I'm still passionate about ministry and academia. But what I learned was that these distinct pathways were not for me. They ran against the grain of my own soul. I didn't recognize it. I didn't want to recognize it at the time. But now I do.

My summer reading reminded me what I was wired for. Interestingly, this was hard-wired into me long before I met Christ. Looking back, I am now beginning to see how his calling on my life is a continuation of who he made me to be. I am living more deeply into how I am, how I'm wired, and what I long for.

I need a frontier.

My hunch is that you do as well.

That's why you picked up this book. That's why we pick up any book for that matter. The title and summary strike a chord. We resonate with them. We're compelled to investigate more fully.

My fearful observation in regards to church planting is that it is rarely an adventuresome or pioneering endeavor. Instead, it is a massive industrial machine replete with so-called sages, events, conferences, books, and massive funding. It is the new Silicon Valley of ministry. Many planters embark as if they were venture capitalists. Both investors and planters are hoping for the same things ... a great return on investment.

For many church planters, it is a strategic career move. No one will really admit it. There's no way anyone would say it out loud or even admit it to their closest confidants. We deceive ourselves and are afraid to admit it. What we ultimately hope for is a big and growing church, a level of financial independence and fruit from our efforts, and, if it's not asking too much, maybe a little notoriety too. Yeah, that's always nice.

The machine churns on. We could argue church planting has been industrialized in North America. Denominations are in the widget-making enterprise with uniform training, metrics, and the like. Planters, like unformed lumps of raw material, are honed, fashioned, and trimmed to fit into the mold of their denomination or network.

In other words, the pioneers and explorers have been domesticated.

I've spent the last ten-plus years noticing myself becoming pretty disillusioned with this machinery. I didn't want anything to do with it. I thought I was done. Ministry over. Calling voided. I did my time, put in my service, and was honorably discharged. Time to move on with my life. But the pilot light of my soul never turned off.

What I've come to realize had happened to me was actually the domestication of my own sense of calling and vocation. Sure, the machinery still exists. Lots of great things are happening for others as a result. Praise be to God. It just wasn't for me. I realized that as soon as a place was "found" or "discovered," my heart was already moving on towards new frontiers and vistas.

I have to imagine this was the same impetus that compelled eighteen-year-old

Everett Ruess to embark on his personal journey to live in the harsh landscape of the American Southwest in the 1930s. He eschewed the safe and normal life to instead live as a vagabond. We see the same in Chris McCandless of *Into the Wild* fame. And we see it in the life of one of my favorite writers, Edward Abbey. For long stretches he'd live alone as a park ranger or atop a fire lookout. Although highly educated and an accomplished writer, he jettisoned it all to live a life free and on the edge. These were all pioneers and explorers in their own right.

I'm convinced that for some remarkably glorious reason, a certain percentage of the population is simply wired this way. Was it simply genetics? A pivotal life experience early on? I can only surmise, but that's why I am drawn to writers such as these ... because they are kindred spirits. While none of these men would self-identify as followers of Christ, we are still cut out of the same cloth. I have the added perspective of a life set free by the blood of

Christ. As a result, this whole sense of pioneering and exploring is not a pursuit of self or some narcissistic fascination with me. Instead, it's living a life for others.

Interestingly enough, when I do so, it feeds my soul. Why? Because I'm living the life God has wired me for. I give in. I surrender. I cannot live wearing other peoples' masks.

I have to imagine that it was this same hard-wiring that drove so many throughout the centuries to forgo comfort and ease to instead live life on the edge. Some were being reckless. Others did it for altruistic motives.

For a couple years, I took the deep dive into the life of Father Francisco Eusebio Kino, a seventeenth-century Jesuit missionary. He could've lived a life of ease in Europe's cloistered halls of academia. Instead, he boarded a ship destined for New Spain. While he dreamed of ultimately reaching Asia, he was assigned to what is today northern Mexico and Arizona. As a frontier pioneer missionary, he left a lasting legacy that's still felt today.

How many of us are like that? Most of us hit that crossroads. A life of safety, comfort, and ease. It could be on staff at a large church where life is cushy ... and mundane. Uninspiring. Or you're working at a job in sales and you're really good at it. You do well. You live comfortably. Your house is paid for. You vacation in all of the cool places. But you want more. You realize you don't want to live life only for a few moments of relaxation a few weeks out of the year. You want more. Now.

I see it all the time in one of the courses I teach. Since it's an accelerated degree program for working adults, the students tend to be older. The storyline is all too common. Started college right after high school. Quit. Hated it. Got addicted. Didn't know what to do. Got into a relationship. Got pregnant. And a million other reasons. Regardless of why, most stopped going to school. Now in their 30s, 40s, and 50s, they are sick of life kicking the crap out of them. They want a degree and to do something with their lives.

That's the common narrative of all this. Purpose. Meaning. Living a life that counts. We'd trade almost anything for that.

I became part of the church planting machinery. My soul shriveled. Church planting was taken out of the hands of the pioneers and explorers and placed into the hands of bureaucrats and people who love spreadsheets. It was tamed. Neutered. Domesticated.

I moved to and plopped into the middle of what I was told was the last frontier of missions in North America ... the Pacific Northwest. That couldn't have been farther from the truth. After ten years here, I began my own quest, a journey, an expedition if you will, to discover where the frontier truly is. Rather than being in some far-off exotic place, it wasn't where I thought it would be. Once I found it I realized then and there that only explorers, pioneers, and misfits would ever want to go.

Welcome to the frontier.

I think that's what is common among pioneers and explorers. That sense or compulsion to go where the crowds are not. When it comes to church planting, the crowds in Portland might as well be Disneyland. It's the same impulse that keeps intrepid souls away from well-trafficked state parks and national monuments. Instead, what is truly inspiring for them is to grab a map and head off into those places where most don't go ... because they don't even know they exist.

Those places dot our maps. Out West due to our massive and expansive geography they are often times far removed and isolated. It could be a small mining community of 2,450 people, a backwoods higher-elevation town of 750 souls, or a small border city with 16,000 residents. Places that only pioneers and explorers want to go to. Most everyone else opts for cool and appealing cities.

Up until this point, I've lumped explorers and pioneers into the same category. In reality they are two completely different kinds of people. Both have unique skills that are needed. But they are as different from one another as can be.

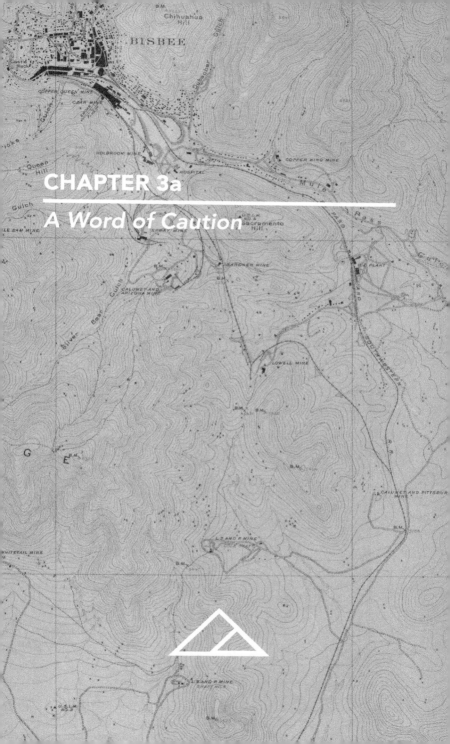

CHAPTER 3a

A Word of Caution

Explorers explore. Simple enough, right? They are cutting new trails, venturing into new terrain, and uncovering what was once lost or forgotten or overlooked.

We may in our mind think of the mountain men of old pushing westward following game trails and trapping for animal pelts. Obviously, this term is nuanced as it is applicable from the vantage point of the one setting out on the journey. Yes, Coronado explored. He led his expedition across thousands of miles of terrain on foot and horseback. He was exploring territory that was "virgin" *to him*. We know he came across multiple Pueblo villages that had existed for a couple hundred years. Prior to them were the small villages and cities, such as in Chaco Canyon, left by the Anasazi.

If we're playing settlers-versus-explorers, in this case Coronado was the explorer and the Pueblo people were the settlers, as they had been rooted in place for generations. That reveals the storyline and the reality of this whole conversation. Exploring is simply coming across what is new *to you*.

My exploration of the mountains of southern Arizona looking for traces of the Hohokam people who "disappeared" between 500 and 600 years ago is an example of this tension. I'd venture down trails or washes, peer under trees and bushes, and step off the path to look for pottery shards and foundation stones from the walls and pit-houses of the Hohokam. I learned to be pretty good at spotting pottery along the way.

To me, I was exploring. In reality I was perusing what was once the homes of people who lived there long before me. But from *my* vantage point, I was exploring. What that means is often times the frontier is what is just beyond our experience and knowledge. It might as well be blank spots on the map. The problem, though, as I mentioned before, is when you think you've uncovered something new only to find out many others are already there doing the same thing.

That's how I view church planting today in many cities. Many church planters arrive thinking or believing they are explorers only to realize that there have been wave after wave of contemporary church planters there before them. It's no different than prospecting for gold. When someone finds the mother lode, a rich vein of that elusive and expensive mineral, then miners and dreamers from all over the world leave it all to move there in hopes of wealth and glory.

Many leave jobs, wives, and children to make it rich. Relational and financial collateral damage are assumed for many. They hop on ships, buy mules and supplies, and trek deep into the wilderness towards their future ... only to find that by the time they get there, it's all been mined out. They missed it. I have to speculate that deep down many church planters I meet feel the same. While they didn't leave their wives and children behind, they journeyed far from homes, extended family, and safety for this new frontier. They sold houses, left jobs, and so on, as they journeyed into this new land, this new city. But once they get there, they realize it has all been mined out.

All of the low-hanging fruit ... unchurched Christians or even churched Christians ... have already been swept up into other new churches. Any hopes of explosive growth, stardom, and "making it" ebb away just like the hopes of the prospector when he realized he's too late. Often times a planter will move into a neighborhood only to find out five established churches and four new church plants are already there.

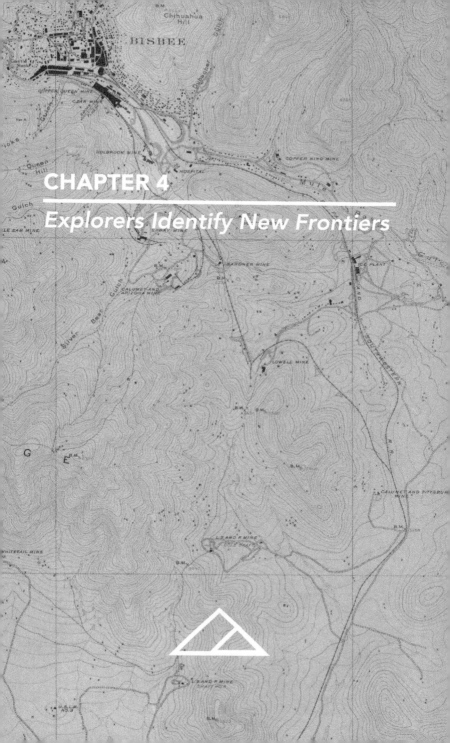

CHAPTER 4

Explorers Identify New Frontiers

For the longest time, I struggled to identify who I was in light of any sense of calling or vocation. I was an artist and deeply curious. Then I came to faith in Christ and it seemed as though they didn't quite fit in all the spiritual-gifts tests I took. In the same way that I got rid of all my "secular" CDs, I was encouraged to make a clean break from my past and just give my life to Jesus.

Since I didn't know any better, it's what I did. I stopped being me and simply tried to fit into the new community I found myself in. Then when I transferred to a Christian university, my insecurities only deepened. I felt like I didn't fit it or belong. It's not that I was a rebel or anything, I just didn't grow up in that world. I had to adopt a whole new language, culture, and customs.

So I continued on that path after college going on staff at two different churches. At this point I was immersed and had shed much of who I was. I didn't know any better, but as time went on there was a growing dissonance. That all changed when I stepped into church planting. My whole world transformed. For the first time I was consciously blending together the worlds of my loves, interests, passions, and personality with the special or specific calling God had on my life.

To be fair, I don't blame anyone for my previous misunderstandings of the new world I stepped into once I became a Christian. It's not like anyone said I needed to act like this or that. I simply tried to fit in. I wasn't good at it. I wasn't some loose cannon, rebellious, and chaffing under my newfound faith in Christ. I was just a college dude trying to figure things out as a new Christian.

Douglas Schuurman in *Vocation: Discerning Our Callings in Life* brings together the worlds of natural abilities, spiritual gifts, and calling / vocation in a way I haven't seen before. When I read his words, the light clicked on.

> Though the New Testament speaks of these gifts and callings as "spiritual" gifts given through the grace and acted upon in faith, they are related to the natural abilities of the members who receive and utilize them. Saul's intelligence, passion, and comprehensive grasp of the Hebrew Bible and Jewish tradition were not cancelled by his call and callings. Rather they were redirected and transformed into fruitful service to the church and the world. The spiritual gift, and its related calling, brings something genuinely new to an existing individual, but assessing natural gifts can help in the discernment of spiritual gifts and related callings. *The redeeming God who calls to new service is the same God*

> who created and providentially situated a
> person in her places of responsibility.[1]

God made me to be me. God made you to be you. None of us chose our personality, likes, interests, and leanings. More than that, we didn't choose where we grew up, how we grew up, nor our parents. These all combined to form who we are today. Christ's call on our lives does not negate this. If anything, it adds fuel to the fire.

This has relevance to the conversation of explorers, pioneers, and misfits. Those with this predisposition are simply wired this way because that is how they were born. When it comes to misfits, I use that term to denote those who regularly applies divergent thinking. They swim against the stream. They see both the world and the solutions to problems differently. That's why they are essential in the mission of the church.

---

[1] Schuurman, *Vocation*, 38-39. Italics mine.

Beginning with this chapter, I will look at each of these types of people that are gifts to the church. In doing so, I will not fall along the neat and tidy lines of spiritual gifts assessments or APEST[2] types. While I would assume they would all fit under the umbrella of apostolic types, I want to instead focus more on their functions. Will that spill over into APEST and other gifts tests? Yes. And it will also spill over into other assessments and tests whether StrengthsFinder, Enneagram, DISC, Myers-Briggs, and more.

While explorers, pioneers, and misfits may seem to be different labels to describe the same people, that is not the case. The impulse to be an explorer, while similar, is different than that of a pioneer. Interrelated but different. The misfit attribute probably does apply to both the pioneer and the explorer. With that said, let's dive in.

---

[2] APEST = Apostle, Prophet, Evangelist, Shepherd, Teacher.

Stewart Udall in his magnificent book that I shared about in chapter 3, *Majestic Journey*, about the life and journey of Francisco Vásquez de Coronado, the sixteenth-century Spanish conquistador, details the explorer ethos of Spain and Portugal during this era. In particular, what Spain accomplished will never be replicated.

> In all the annals of exploration, there is no year that has the luster of 1542. No one in Seville planned it that way, but 1542 was the great climax of the Spanish age of discovery—a year in which Spain had expeditions under way that stretched halfway around the globe in a vast circle from California to Kansas to North Carolina to the Amazon River to the pampas of Southern Brazil to Chile's Atacama Desert to Luzon, in the newly named Philippine Islands, and back across the Pacific to the shores of Oregon.[3]

---

[3] Udall, *Majestic Journey*, 31.

Those plucky Spaniards explored the ends of the earth, whether on foot or by sea. They were explorers to the core.

Again, tension noted. I felt that tension when describing the exemplary life of Father Francisco Eusebio Kino, the seventeenth-century Jesuit missionary in what is today Sonora, Mexico and Arizona, in my book *Intrepid: Navigating the Intersection of Church Planting + Social Entrepreneurship.* Kino's work as a pioneer missionary priest went hand-in-hand with Spain's exploration, expansion, and colonization. Tension felt and acknowledged.

With that said, the explorer ethos of Spain was second to none. In fact, in light of today's immigration debates and the growing segment of white nationalism, Udall shows us the benefit of reminding one another of our Spanish origins. "With the Hispanic segment of our population increasing each year, the gains would be substantial if we had the wit to widen our horizons and pluck our Spanish century from the wastebasket of history."[4] He continues:

> To be sure, such a reorientation would involve some lowered profiles and create a few pockets of distress. But truth often offers compensations that assuage pain. Would our self-esteem be diminished, for example, if we were to admit that Daniel Boone discovered nothing? Or to conclude that the country Lieutenant Zebulun Pike "discovered" in 1805 had been a stomping ground for Spaniards since the 1540s? Or to acknowledge that the self-styled "Great Pathfinder," General John C. Frémont, did not "open the West" but, rather, followed trails blazed by Spaniards and white Indians who called themselves mountain men?
>
> The story of the American frontier will have a different flavor if we decide to add a dash and spice of Spain's sixteenth century. And our ethos will surely be magnified if we have the *Mayflower* folk move over and allow the authentic first families of our sixteenth century to share their symbolic

---

[4] Ibid., 140.

front-row pew at our national processionals.[5]

One can argue that this explorer ethos has been what this continent was founded on. And I'm not even talking about life after Contact, but what we now refer to as pre-Columbian America. Long before the first Europeans, those of Athapascan descent migrated from Canada to the Southwest to eventually become knowns as the Navajos and Apaches. Long before them were the Anasazi, Hohokam, and Mogollon. All of the cliff dwellings, great houses, and artifacts that dot the Navajo Nation were already abandoned by the time the Navajo arrived around 1400.

In other words, these explorations had nothing to do with a white European tradition. Instead, the explorer tradition is as old as humanity. One can argue it began the day when Adam and Eve left the Garden. It happened when Cain killed Abel and was

---

[5] Ibid., 142.

banished to be a wanderer. His migration outward chronicled the founding of the first city mentioned in Scripture.

These examples bring up our tenuous relationship with the word "explorer." Depending on its usage and application the meaning can range from fun, invigorating, and life-giving at one extreme to ravaging, pillaging, and destruction at the other. It probably doesn't need to be mentioned, but how I choose to use the word embraces hope and optimism.

To explore means to seek out and uncover what is new *to you*. As I mentioned above, the exploring and pioneering Athapascans (Navajos, Apache, etc.) were exploring new (to them) territory when they descended into the American Southwest. They settled in an area that was previously lived in and then abandoned by the "Old Ones" (Anasazi).

In all of my journeys and explorations in my own small world, I am constantly reminded that what I uncover and see is really only new to me. But that does not diminish the excitement of this discovery process. In my mind I truly am on the frontier ... and I am. It is the frontier of my own experiences and imagination. Besides, are there really any places left that have not been trekked through and explored by at least *someone*? Probably not. Sure, not every place has undergone the same level of documentation and mapping, but someone has been there.

Last night I started reading *The Lost City of the Monkey God*. It's about finding the "White City" in a remote mountainous jungle in Honduras. While the story of the book is packed with mystery, intrigue, and discovery, the reality is we're talking about a pre-Columbian city that remains buried under dense foliage. However, to the outsiders trekking and hacking deep into the inhospitable jungle, it is as new to them as when humans first set foot on the moon.

Explorers explore.

They seek out new terrain and experiences. They are not content with the status quo or the routine of a "normal" life. Their fires are not lit unless they are on the edge. This doesn't mean all explorers are irresponsible ruffians who don't or can't work at a normal job. What it does mean, though, is that if in some capacity they are not exploring and pushing back on the blank spots on their maps, their souls begin to shrivel.

Learning and discovery are what drive them.

This also doesn't mean they are constantly globe-trotting to far-off places around the world. There's a lifetime of adventure right out our front door. I realize that the longer I live in Oregon and the Pacific Northwest. As time moves forward a growing awareness develops of how little I truly know about this place. I felt the same in Arizona. There's always a new wrinkle in the landscape I have not seen nor explored. It could be a ridge line, a canyon, a river, a coastal beach, or neighborhoods throughout Portland. It makes my head spin at the possibilities. I want to get out and explore.

That's also why I tend to get bored with routine. At the same time, ironically, I love routine. It fits my personality. I need it. I do the same thing every morning when I wake up. Make a cup of coffee either via pourover or aeropress. I then spend time reading the Bible, journaling, and praying. Then I will read and spend time writing (like now). I need that to ground me. I fumble along without a routine.

However, I get bored with too much routine in the places I go. For example, once I hop off writing this morning I'm loading up my bike to go mountain biking in Hood River. On the one hand I'm looking forward to it. On the other there's a yawning apathy because it's a trail system (Syncline) that I've ridden countless times. It's a good workout and a chance to go riding. It is not exploring and going on a daring journey by any stretch.

So how does this notion of explorer fit into the world of the church, church planting, and missionary work? It's probably not shocking to say this, but I think we already know. It's pretty obvious. These are the bona fide apostolic types. Pioneering new terrain.

The challenge before us though, particularly in the West ... not only in the West in regards to a Euro-American framework, but West as in the Western United States, ... is that is there anything really *new* anymore? You see, and I'll get into this later, the progression goes like this. Explorers explore new terrain. Pioneers come on the heels of explorers and begin carving out a new life on the frontier (explorers have already moved on), and then the settlers come once the land has been found, civilized, domesticated, or however we want to say it. Again, it's highly contentious to use those words because of the ethnocentric framework from which it stems. But I am speaking of broad generalities.

So if there's no new frontier than who is an explorer? Also, does that mean all explorers have vanished? No longer needed? Of this I am convinced ... the frontier is not static. Never has been. It's always on the move. Again, that means multiple storylines are happening simultaneously. When the United States was pushing westward into *their* new frontier, they came, for example, to an area now called Arizona in which lived numerous distinct tribes of Apaches, Navajos, Hopi, Yavapai, Tohono O'odham, and more. If we think it was some serene setting, we need to be reminded that often times even different Apache tribes were at war with each other ... Tonto against Chiricahua, etc.

The frontier has shifted and continues to do so. What appealed to me about the urban core of the city fifteen years ago was that in many ways for me it was a new frontier. As a former church planting strategist, it finally dawned on me at that time there was very little church planting in the city center. Most new churches were being started in the suburbs. That drove me to the city to walk, explore, pray, and ultimately fall in love with.

Then the winds of change shifted.

Fast forward the storyline and the city center in all cities is now *the* place for church planting. Once the explorers did their work, then came the pioneers, and then the settlers.

A few years ago, I wrote the book *Urban Hinterlands: Planting the Gospel in Uncool Places*. It was the most difficult book for me to write on an emotional level. Why? Because I was almost afraid of what was happening to me. I had fallen out of love with the city, particularly urban cores. What happened?

The frontier changed. Deep down I had sensed it but couldn't put it into words. The urban core went from new frontier to now very much settled. It went from fringe to mainstream in terms of church planting. From having little to no emphasis on planting there to now a flash flood torrent of church planters moving in.

It was akin to explorers pushing deep into uncharted territory. Once they found it they marveled at its beauty and hung around for a little bit. Then one day they noticed on the next ridge over the campfire of another explorer. The following week there were three other campfires on adjacent ridges. Pretty soon there was a low-hanging cloud of smoke hovering over the valley like a wet blanket. The campfires were too many to count and the noise was deafening. That's what I felt was happening to the city and church planting there.

And so my heart left.

I began searching for new vistas ... new frontiers. Then I found it. I realized it had been there all along, but frontiers shift. When we think we are moving into some new territory that was previously unknown, that's when the realization hits that we're not the first ones there.

Charles Mann, in his groundbreaking book *1491: New Revelations of the Americas Before Columbus*, points out that the Western Hemisphere was not some backwoods Eden inhabited by poverty-stricken indigenous tribes. In fact, the continent was filled with tens of millions of inhabitants who had tamed wildernesses, built breathtaking cities and urban infrastructure on par with the Romans and Egyptians, and housed advanced civilizations. He notes:

> Advertisements still celebrate nomadic, ecologically pure Indians on horseback chasing bison in the Great Plains of North America, but at the time of Columbus the great majority of Native Americans could be found south of the Rio Grande. They were not nomadic, but built up and lived in some of the world's biggest and most opulent cities. Far from being dependent on big-game hunting, most Indians lived on farms. Others subsisted on fish and shellfish. As for the horses, they were from Europe, except for llamas in the Andes, the Western Hemisphere had no beasts of burden. In other words, the Americas were immensely busier, more diverse, and more populous than researches had previously imagined.

And older too.[6]

---

6 Mann, *1491*, 18.

As Mann argues throughout the book, one people's frontier was another's home. The same is true today for exploring new missionary frontiers. The frontier boundaries are dynamic not static and constantly on the move.

Explorers are searching for these new vistas and frontiers. They are restless until they find them. But what happens when the frontier has shifted? More than ever I am convinced it has. Do you see it? Do you notice?

The new frontier looks something like this ... these are the places and people that have been overlooked and left off the map when it comes to missions and church planting strategy. Oh, no one means to. It's not some grand conspiracy theory. It just happens.

There's a common theme for these types of places and people. They never make any top-10 list of livable places. More than likely the people themselves are not trendy. But when it comes to missions and church planting, they simply are left off the table of strategy.

They are in the in-between places. But isn't that the nature of frontiers? These are the places that most people don't really want to go to until a settlement has been established and safety is ensured. That's what pioneers do.

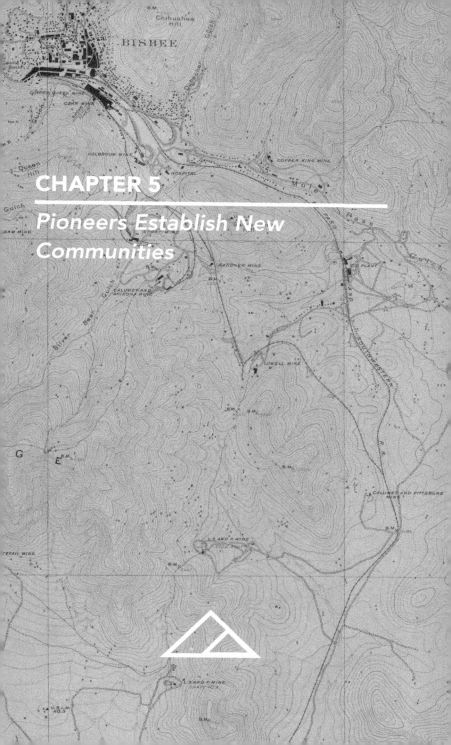

CHAPTER 5

Pioneers Establish New Communities

I've chosen to distinguish explorers from pioneers. While often used interchangeably, they are actually two unique groups of people. Explorers explore. Pioneers come on the heels of explorers and move in. Explorers keep going and push through the ever-changing boundaries and borders.

Borders fascinate me. These arbitrary lines on the map can make or break the opportunities in one's life. Being born a mere twenty feet this way or that can impact your family for generations. Even then at times borders around you can change. Think about citizens of Mexico in what is today Arizona or California. Those states used to be part of Mexico. Your family lived there for generations. Mexican citizens. One day a treaty was signed on the other side of the continent and all of a sudden, you're now a resident of the United States. You didn't move. The border did.

I think of other groups like the Chiricahua Apache. Why are they in Oklahoma? As they were the last holdouts to have been forced onto the reservation system they were punished for generations to come. Ripped from their homeland, placed on trains, and transported east. Initially they were relegated to Florida. Many died. Ultimately, they were placed in Oklahoma which is a far cry from their ancestral homes among the Dragoon Mountains and the other sky islands in Southeast Arizona.

Borders are real. Boundaries influence both our lives and generations to come. When it comes to new land, new terrain, and new territory, there are always explorers who go first. They scope out the land, assess, map, take notes, and scout. They in turn return back home and report what they have seen. Good land. Ample water. Numerous sites for raising crops. Plenty of game for hunting. If you think this was simply what happened when white Americans moved into the West you're gravely mistaken. This was the same process for any migratory group of people.

Those of Athapascan descent must've sent scouts ahead, explored, and reported back in order for the rest of the people to eventually migrate from what is now Canada to the American Southwest. In the early twentieth century, there must've been forerunners or scouts who reported back to African Americans in the South of all of the manufacturing jobs in the cities of the north. That began what we now call the Great Migration. Millions of blacks moving to cities like Chicago, Pittsburgh, Milwaukie, and Cleveland to take jobs in the steel industry, auto manufacturing, and more.

Explorers see new frontiers and report back. Then comes the pioneers. Whereas explorers are more nomadic and constantly on the move, pioneers forged ahead into this new land or city to carve out a new life for themselves. Often at great sacrifice and even peril. The history of settlement on this continent is this very story. Whether we're talking about people migrating tens of thousands of years ago (whether by land bridge or boat) to Spaniards in the 16th century to French fur trappers floating down the Ohio and Mississippi rivers to establish settlements like Dubuque, Iowa; Cape Girardeau, Missouri or New Orleans, Louisiana, pioneers establish colonies.

Explorers explore. Pioneers establish new communities. Settlers then come in and populate and further the establishment. All are needed and essential. The key is understanding who you are. It took me years before I realized I am more of an explorer than anything else. That's probably why it chafes me living in Portland. It's a hotspot and hub for church planting. It's trendy to plant here. It's trendy to plant trendy churches here. It's trendy to plant trendy churches here for trendy people. I need a new frontier.

But not everyone is like that. I get it. Like anything, it's a gift and a curse. Never content. Always wanting more. New places. New experiences. I sometimes joke that I was born in the wrong century. Give me blank spaces on the map. But the reality is there are still plenty on my own personal map. And so I explore.

However, if the world was full of explorers it would be a mess. An utter disaster. We'd probably go back to being nomads and subsistence farmers. Cities are truly a gift. That's where pioneers come and begin turning chaos into order. Settlements are established. Communities are formed. Crops are planted. Schools are created. Businesses pop up. Before we realize what happened it went from an idea to a town ... and eventually (possibly) a city. The explorer saw the terrain and reported back. The pioneer came in and carved a new community out of the wilderness. That happened in Portland and it happened in Cahokia, the ancient city just east of present-day St. Louis that peaked at around 35,000 people before its demise in the 15th century before European colonization.

Pioneers are the tip of the spear. They go in where previously no one wants to go. Think of the landscape across our continent today. Where are all of those places that no one wants to go? I have a list. It is full of names of communities you've never heard of. Most haven't. It's not Portland, Seattle, San Francisco, or other big cities. They are smaller communities neglected and overlooked. But their problem is they are not appealing, desirous, nor trendy. It could be a *colonia* along the US-Mexico border, a ranching community in eastern Oregon, or a low-income neighborhood in your city.

As I've explained at length, talking of explorers, settlers, creating settlements and communities ... colonizing ... is a contentious analogy. It should be. Rightly so. That's why history serves us well. We can look back and see over and over where people have done it wrong. Europeans did it wrong. Africans did it wrong. Indigenous Americans did it wrong. History is littered with conquest, subjugation, slavery, and slaughter.

Sometimes ignorance is bliss. The more we know, the more pain we feel when we read about grievances and difficult chapters in the history of humanity. Last night as I was reading *Once They Moved Like the Wind: Cochise, Geronimo, and the Apache Wars* by David Roberts, I was struck by the back-and-forth tit-for-tat cruelty between the Apache and Mexicans in Chihuahua and Sonora. After a particularly fierce battle where most of the Chihenne (a band within the Chiricahua Apache) warriors were killed by a collection of Mexican soldiers and citizens, the remaining hundred Apache women and children were sold into slavery. Over the next eighteen months, the Apache, led by the aging Nana, would retaliate by slaughtering Mexican ranchers and even whole towns. The parched desert soaked up much blood in the late 1800s.

When I write of explorers and pioneers, I do not do so from some elitist framework birthed out of superiority, conquest, and domination. Instead, from a framework—a posture—marked by humility, love, and servanthood. Yes, it *is* possible to be an explorer as well as a pioneer in a healthy, life-giving, endearing, and dignified manner. We see this theme repeatedly across the pages of the New Testament. Whether from the lips of Jesus or from the pen of Paul to the church in Rome, we're reminded that we're to love our neighbors as ourselves.

I too had read that over and over in the New Testament. So many times that I've become too accustomed—even numb—to the potency of those words. When we ask one simple follow-up question, it changes the whole narrative of our how we're to live and act. Couple that with this conversation of explorers and pioneers we have a clear roadmap of how we're to enter into new communities.

That question is: What does it mean to love our neighbor? What does that even look like? Obviously, it doesn't mean simply to love those we like to hang around with. Then Jesus does the unthinkable. He tells a story to demonstrate who our neighbor is. To the Jews it was those dreaded Samaritans. Two thousand years removed, we don't get the scandal of that example. That would be like telling the Apache to love and serve the residents of Sonora as *greater* than themselves. Today that would be telling conservative Republican politicians to love and serve the immigrant family fleeing for their lives from Guatemala.

But Jesus' story of the "good Samaritan" was more than that. They hero was not the Jew, but the Samaritan. Set among my previous examples, it would be the story of a wounded Apache warrior who was rescued and nursed back to health by the citizen of one of the communities that the Apaches had razed. It would be the conservative Republican politician on vacation to San Carlos, Mexico. On the drive down at a gas station, he is robbed, beaten to the edge of death, driven out of town and dumped into the desert. Then a group of immigrants walking from Guatemala to the US border find him, know who is he, and even though he staunchly opposed immigration and he supported families being separated at the border, they still had compassion on him. They carried him back into town, used what little money they had to take him to the hospital and get him the care he needed.

This is the scandal of grace and the gospel.

We enter as pioneers into new communities with that same posture. It can be done. It doesn't have to be about conquest, superiority, or even the removal of people from their homes. To come ... serve ... and give our lives away for the betterment of these people and communities whether in the city or rural communities.

Again, we have an amazing example in Jesus. The doctrine of the incarnation is more than figuring out what exactly happened when divinity entered humanity and when Jesus took on flesh and blood and entered the world through the womb of a teenage girl. More scandals at hand than we realize in what we now call the Christmas story.

First there was the announcement. God— the creator of the cosmos—was soon to be born. Flesh and blood. The news was given to a dumbfounded unwed teen. She would carry the Savior in her womb and give birth to him.

More scandals continued to happen. Those who received the news were astrologers from the east. They traveled great distances and brought gifts of celebration for the birth of the Messiah. King Herod catches wind and in order to defend his position, he opts to slaughter all male children two years old and under in Bethlehem. A clean sweep.

On the night of Jesus' birth, the announcement came. More scandal. The news was delivered to illiterate shepherds. The lowest of the low. They were recipients of the greatest news in human history. God was here. Among us. Nearby in a borrowed barn in a feed trough.

If there ever was a posture that was bold enough to adapt and serve as a framework for pioneers, it was and is Jesus. To force the analogy, he was an explorer and pioneer. But he didn't come as a mighty conquistador subjugating, raping, and slaughtering as he went. He came to serve and give his life as a ransom.

We don't have to be fretful about embracing life as an explorer or pioneer. It actually *can* be done in a life-giving and endearing way that is not about changing culture or displacement. If only more (white) church planters would adopt this ethos when moving into gentrifying neighborhoods. Again,

Jesus serves as a great example in terms of culture and adaptation.

Philip Yancey, in his book *The Jesus I Never Knew*, makes the argument that we can't understand Jesus without making sense of his Jewishness. Jesus was born as a first-century Jew. He took on the ethnicity and culture of the Jews. He wasn't an *acultural* being but adapted and adopted the culture, lifestyle, patterns, and habits of other Jews. He went to the temple, paid taxes, observed the religious celebrations, and the like.

Pioneers moving into new communities ought not to come in with some cultural superiority seeking to simply wipe the slate clean and change everything. What is remarkable about the people and place you're moving into? How do you incarnate yourself in that community and become an insider? I'm not saying that process is quick or easy. It could be a lifetime of work simply to be accepted. In cities like Portland, it takes no time since most are outsiders as well. In smaller tight-knit communities this process can take years ... even decades.

Yes, I took a lot of time to lay that foundation that one can be a pioneer and do so in a life-giving way that adds value to the community. At times, outside perspectives are what is needed to push the envelope for innovation, growth, and redevelopment. Don't doubt that you can be an asset to the community, whether it's big or small.

Establishing New Communities

When we look at the work of church planting, community development, and social entrepreneurship inevitably we're talking about creating and establishing something new—a new spiritual community, business, non-profit, and more. I use the term "community" loosely to incorporate these various categories from church planting to startups. It certainly entails the formation of a new spiritual community known as the church. In the world of church planting, that can look like several different options.

The first involves bringing a core group of pioneers to relocate with you. You're collectively a group of outsiders. But you're coming in sharing and living out good news. This is no different than what we see of the work of (St.) Patrick in Ireland and how he went about church planting. Bringing a group of outsiders in can be a mixed bag. In cities it goes pretty much unnoticed since most everyone else are transplants. The smaller the community, the more noticeable it is.

As much as you try to come in with a posture of humility and servanthood, not everyone will be excited you're there. I'm talking about other local churches that may perceive you as a threat. Yes, we both know it shouldn't be that way. It happens all the time in cities when various planters relocate in the same neighborhood. There's often an underlying tension between church planters and the pastors of established churches. They just need to admit it, be open about it, address it, and seek to be a blessing to one another.

Moving in as part of a group can be healthy in that it gives the planter shared leadership and a workforce from the get-go. But it can also be unhealthy, as coming in with already established relationships may cause locals difficulty breaking into. Not all groups are equal because not all towns, villages, or cities are the same. In some places, as I've shared, it wouldn't even be noticeable, while in other smaller towns it could be overwhelming for the locals if not done properly.

But this is what pioneers do. They forge ahead into the spaces on the map that most others don't really want to go. As to the reasons why most planters don't go to the blank spots, there are a myriad ranging from the communities being low-income, unsightly, geographically isolated, too small, too parochial, and many more. Pioneers know this going in and (hopefully) plan for it. They actually know these things quite well ... which is *why* they are going. Pioneers pioneer.

For those early pioneers, buying lots when Portland was just a clearing in the thick rain-drenched forest on the west bank of the Willamette River was a far cry from the industrial cities back east from which they came (Boston, New York, etc.). But someone always has to go first or at least early on. That's what pioneers do. They may not have discovered anything themselves but they were some of the very first ones to move in specifically to plant a church, start a business, or launch a non-profit. Bringing a team in from the outside certainly helps.

Then there are pioneers who simply come alone. We've heard it called "parachute church planting" where the planter simply drops into a new town or city all alone, except perhaps for family members. It is akin to paratroopers parachuting in at night while on a dangerous mission.

The first time I planted a church I moved in with a team. It was great having instant leaders and workers to share the ministry with. The second time we planted we simply parachuted in. It's not that we didn't want a team ... we didn't have one. When this happens, the pioneer planter has a long road ahead establishing a new spiritual community literally from scratch. But for those wired that way it is a blessing, a challenge, and truly exhilarating. Hopefully your denomination or church planting network has the patience to let you do this organically, knowing this is a long-term process. But since most don't have that patience, church planters end up grabbing Christians from other local churches. Tension and competition ensue ...

While we lump explorers and pioneers into the same apostolic category, I believe they would be better served if they were kept separate. I understand I'm creating subcategories not found in Acts. I suppose we could point to some of the different attributes of those involved in the different missionary or church-planting journeys. Paul was an explorer and Timothy and Titus were pioneers. It helps to separate them out because it reflects our divergent leanings and inclinations under the apostolic umbrella. In other words, put ten apostolic types in one room and, based on personality type, natural giftings, upbringing, experience, and exposure, they're all going to go about it in different ways. I affirm them. Besides, we're not all cut from the same cloth. That's why we need misfits.

Through Barren Wastelands

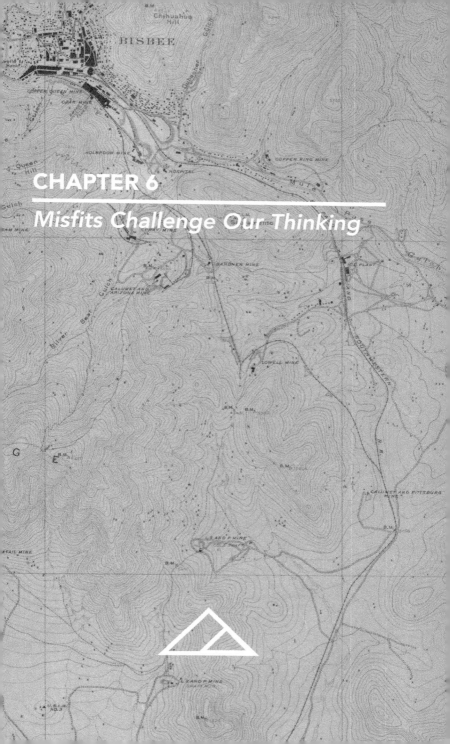

CHAPTER 6
Misfits Challenge Our Thinking

It's September 2019 when I'm writing this. By far my favorite time of the year. The weather has cooled and the rain which the Pacific Northwest is known for has been creeping back. Contrary to popular perceptions, summers here are hot and dry. We'll go weeks—months—without noticeable rain. But that has all changed now.

We're two weeks into the college football season. By far my favorite sport. UCLA is off to an 0-2 start. Why is that a big deal? Because the two teams they lost to are not part of major athletic conferences like UCLA is in (the Pac-12). But it is more than that. *Much* more.

The Bruins are now led by second-year head coach Chip Kelly. If the name doesn't resonate, it's probably because of how far his star has fallen. Chip was once a revolutionary. A genius nearly unequaled. An outlier. A misfit. He changed the entire landscape of college football and his influence crept even into the stodgy NFL.

For a short span, Chip led the program at the University of Oregon. If you've been to Eugene where the university is located, you quickly realize that this is not a hotbed of top-level football talent. The same phenomenon plagues other schools like Boise State, the University of Wyoming, and more. Isolated and removed from talent pools. As a result, what Chip was able to accomplish is even more astounding.

In his four years as a head coach at Oregon, he went 46-7 and made a trip to the national title game. What is even more remarkable was in the following NFL draft, not one of his players was drafted in the first round. He did it all with seemingly less talented players.

Chip did nothing short of innovate college football. Between the hype uniform combinations, new athletic facilities, an up-tempo offense, and even better nutrition and practice habits, the Oregon Ducks became the gold standard in college football. He was a disruptor. Until the rest of college football caught up. The former innovator and outlier is now struggling.

We've always had disruptors. We need disruptors. When everyone else is going one direction, they push against the grain, swim upstream, and any other analogy that applies. They are gifts and yet many view them as curses. We saw that with Chip Kelly.

Throughout history, disruptors have challenged the status quo ... and often times paid the price with their lives. I'm not talking about anarchy, rebellion, military coups, or anything like that. Instead, disruptors go against conventional wisdom. They say things such as, *Actually, the earth revolves around the sun* (and not the other way around). They make bold proclamations, nail them to the door of a church, and declare how we don't need to pay money as a way to stay out of purgatory. Where would we be without disruptors? They offer course corrections. They point us to either pioneering new terrain or restoring our balance when we've erred in the extreme.

This morning, a different kind of disruption took place. You probably didn't notice it, but I did. It was a small tremor from deep beneath the earth that only registered 1.3 on the Richter Scale. It took place while I was in my classroom. While it wasn't the first of its kind to occur, the voices of my students expressed dismay.

A disruption can be a good thing.

One of the courses I'm teaching this semester is Religion 320 ... Spirituality, Character, and Service. In a nutshell we spend an inordinate amount of time wrestling with calling, vocation, purpose, and meaning. I start off most mornings with a quote that I have up on the screen. The authors of these quotes range from explorers, adventurers, naturalists, theologians, pastors, writers, and the like. The point is to start the class off with discussion around these topics. Also, since it's a 9:00 AM class I need to be proactive to get students engaged.

Today's quote was from a book by Mark Batterson. In *Wild Goose Chase* he writes, "When God puts a passion in your heart, whether it be relieving starvation in Africa or educating children in the inner city or making movies with redemptive messages, that God-ordained passion becomes your responsibility. And you have a choice to make. Are you going to be irresponsibly responsible or responsibly irresponsible?"[7] It's the last line that stirred up conversation.

My students, as I've written about repeatedly come from a wide variety of

---

[7] Batterson, *Wild Goose Chase*, 20.

backgrounds. Over sixty percent of my class are students of color. Half of my class are athletes on scholarship whether soccer, basketball, or softball. The conversation today shifted in and out of various topics that the quote stimulated. Then the conversation turned.

We talked a lot about societal expectations and the "American Dream." Several students began pushing back on the value of a college education. What does it even mean to have a degree and a piece of paper on the wall? Also the reality of graduating with substantial student loan debt with zero guarantees afterwards. *Why a degree? What will it get me? Is all of the debt and time worth it? I can make just as much or more without a degree.*

I see the same headlines all of the time now. Each successive generation is worse off than the previous generations. Higher student debt, higher cost of living, ridiculously expensive real estate, and so on. There was a disruption in class. They were obviously not the first to voice or express concern, but there was a chorus building as the conversation went on. And yet, here we were. They the students. Me the professor. In a classroom. On campus. At a university. Age-old platitudes from me wouldn't suffice at a time like this. You know, the old *education is good for you*. They wanted more than that.

With higher education costs skyrocketing I don't blame them. I'm with them. That's why I dropped out of getting my second doctorate. Once my free tuition dried up, I faced the harsh reality of finishing it with $30-$40K more in student loan debt. I stopped. The investment did not match the opportunities it would give me post-graduation. At that time six years ago, I kept thinking about whether I really need to spend all of the time and money for just a further validation of my worth, expertise, and knowledge? Did I want to play that game any longer? No.

You see, the disruption at hand is all tied to the technological revolution. In other words, because of technology, more and more people can earn a significant livelihood without a degree. A computer, iPhone, and website are all that is needed. So we're left at a crossroad ... play the game or go our own way? We need voices to speak louder and more often into this disruption. It poses a threat to traditional institutions of higher education. We need to deliver the goods in a way that helps students to see and feel that the value of an education goes beyond the paper on the wall.

This is what disruptors do ... they disrupt the status quo. They're misfits in the truest sense. Without them we'd be lost. OK, but how do misfits relate to the apostolic imagination and church planting movements?

First of all, I don't want to misconstrue what I mean by the term misfits. My hunch is that the term lands in one of several ways. For some it speaks of really eccentric people ... and disturbingly so. We know those types. We see them. They seem to be swept up in conspiracy theories. Or the term conjures up images of rebellious teenagers. The ones always getting in trouble. Skipping school to engage in illicit activities. Running from the law. I'm sure there are plenty of other negative responses to that term. I want to spin it forward, as I've attempted thus far in this chapter, to capture this notion of a disruptor. One who lives in the world of divergent thinking.

Think of any industry or even sport. Those who employ divergent thinking are constantly evolving and innovating. In basketball, Steph Curry and the Golden State Warriors changed not just the landscape of the NBA, but basketball everywhere with their use of the three-ball. They almost relegated centers ... those plodding bigs that the NBA was known for ... as almost obsolete. In football, you have early innovators with different offenses like Mike Leach and the Air Raid. He created an offense using spacing to help his highly under-talented teams to be able to compete (and beat) the traditional powers with all of their blue-chip recruits. Leach even fits the narrative of a misfit with his quirky personality and his love for history and books. As recently as a month ago I finished his book about the life of the great Apache warrior Geronimo. He's a misfit in the truest sense.

In terms of church planting and the apostolic imagination, misfits are ones who simply see the world and landscape around them differently. With no desire to keep up with the latest trends on missional geometry and cool charts, instead they are already plowing ahead trying out new ideas and practices. Most often they are so ahead of the curve that many are never found out. It's when people catch wind of the thoughts and ideas of these misfits that they slowly begin adopting and adapting ... and eventually popularizing them. Most people won't know who those original misfits were. Nor do they really want to be known.

If you've been around church planting long enough, you realize eventually that what ultimately is taking place is nothing more than group-think. The same voices speaking at the same conferences and saying the same things year after year. The only difference is they have new books this year they're promoting rather than the ones they (or their ghost writer) wrote last year.

I had taken about a twelve-year break from going to the Exponential Conference in Orlando, Florida. Touted as the biggest church planting conference I have to admit that nothing had really changed after a decade away. Many of the same speakers, same voices, but with newer books. My hunch is that misfits aren't really even on the national radar. Because most don't even know who they are.

We need misfits. We need these disruptors.

In the sequence of explorers and pioneers, I'm not even sure where to place misfits. I'm sure there are plenty who also fit into either camp. I think of my friend Brian. He's a misfit in the truest sense. You don't know him. Most in his city don't know him. Other pastors probably view him at times as a bit contrarian, odd, eccentric, and more. In my mind I see him in a similar light as Bill Belichick, head coach of the New England Patriots of the NFL. Belichick's genius is hidden beneath a veneer of a rough, grumpy man. That's the way I see Brian.

It had been nearly a decade since I had last seen Brian when I emailed him asking to meet up. I was happy when he replied and the appointment was scheduled. Brian pastors a church filled with low-income people on the margins of society, both socially and geographically. Brian himself lives in a double-wide trailer. He's pastored this church with a steady hand for years. No hype. No hoopla. No explosive growth. Just an in-your-face kind of love and leadership.

At the time, I was raising funds to venture out and do Intrepid as my new ministry venture. I didn't want his nor his church's money as much as I wanted his advice and wisdom. If you've followed Intrepid or even read the book, then you know my focus has been and is on planting churches, community development, and startups in overlooked and neglected places among people who're marginalized for a variety of reasons. If Brian planted through us, he'd be the poster child based on where he's pastoring and living out in the desert.

As I shared with him the focus of Intrepid and what I was dreaming of, particularly focusing on lower-income communities, Brian shared a nugget of wisdom that I've been holding in my hand since. Slowly turning it over. As we shared a meal, he paused, leaned toward me, and said, "If you really want to track where the front-edge growth of poor communities are ... follow the Dollar Tree." He went on the explain how the Dollar Tree has it all figured out in terms of demographic trends and changes. They're one step ahead. When a zip code or neighborhood begins spiraling down, that's when they open a store. In other words, the Dollar Tree knows its target market so well that it follows them wherever they are.

Brian's recommendation to me was that wherever you see new Dollar Tree stores opening is where we should focus Intrepid. That was pure genius. I haven't forgotten it. Brian is a misfit. He is needed. You'll never catch Brain up on stage at Exponential. He'll never be invited to lead or teach even one of its workshop or a breakout session. I'm actually convinced that Brian has never even heard of Exponential nor would he go there even if what was an all-expenses-paid trip. That's the thing about misfits. They're not known, sought out, nor really even understood. They border on eccentric.

I'd venture to say all of the current trends that have been popularized, whether within church planting or the culture at large, were pioneered in obscurity by misfits. They weren't trying to be trendsetters or trendy. They simply see the world differently. Also, many of their ideas simply won't become mainstream. Can you imagine a main-stage speaker at Exponential offering the latest church planting strategy by following the trends of where Dollar Trees are opening? Frankly, that's neither cool, trendy, nor sexy. It also won't sell books nor open up the door for speaking engagements. Misfits march by the beat of a different drummer. We desperately need them, their voices, and contributions.

Without misfits, our thinking becomes stuck, insulated, and myopic. Innovation always comes from the margins, not the mainstream. By the time something has become mainstream, the misfits have long since moved on to other ideas and projects. Sometimes they can be too far ahead of the curve. It might even take a generation or two for the rest of us to catch up. Or years later someone stumbles across their writings, art, music, or video clips and at the right time their voices are finally heard.

Obviously with anything, there are unhealthy extremes and dangers. Again, that's not my focus here. I am not saying that something that's not mainstream and obscure always makes it a good idea and should be adopted. Simply because the idea seems far-fetched doesn't mean it's wrong. But it may not be right for a certain place or time.

For this reason, I rarely read any books related to ministry. By the time books get into print, the innovations they put forth have already been popularized and repeated so often that any semblance of newness has long since passed. That is the nature of trends and fads. That's not even a bad thing. Think of how long you hung onto your cargo shorts and resisted going the skinny jeans route. However, by the time you convinced yourself that skinny jeans were finally one fashion trend that you *must* adopt just to at least remotely be "in," the culture and fashion have already moved on. Skinny jeans, although here to stay, have long been relegated to the rear-view mirror like your once beloved cargo shorts.

As a result of trying to keep my ear to the ground, I do my best to read from non-ministry sources. As I shared, I recently finished Mike Leach's book on the life and leadership of the Apache warrior Geronimo. Because Leach draws inspiration from Geronimo and other sources such as pirates, one can see why he's viewed as an offensive genius. He continues to push paradigms and think differently. He's a misfit in the truest sense.

My whole summer's reading has been spent on non-conventional books on "leadership" ... although that is a stretch because the books have nothing overtly to do with the topic. This week I finished *Once They Moved Like Wind* by David Roberts about the Cochise, Geronimo, and the Chiricahua Apaches. Like Leach, I find their story compelling and heart-wrenching. Their ancestral homeland was invaded by white Americans moving in from the east. At first, attempts were made by the Apaches to accommodate and live at peace. But as we know, these tribes and all others were systematically wiped out and forced onto reservations, often times in some of the most inhospitable lands available. One can argue that was one of the earliest attempts at gentrification on our continent, whether we're talking whites moving into minority communities or the forced creation of ghettos (reservations).

To say that Geronimo was a misfit is and is not true. Any sense of him going against the grain was because it had been simply thrust upon him. Frontier life was bloody. There was blood on the hands of all parties ... Americans, Mexicans, and Apaches. What was remarkable was Geronimo's ability to apply divergent thinking to always be two steps ahead of the various armies and posses hunting him down. In one last gasp for freedom, Geronimo and a small band of Apaches escaped captivity. As a result, a huge mob set out to track down a tiny band of warriors, women, and children.

General Miles had launched his grand campaign against the Apache menace. He requested and received two thousand additional soldiers, so that by the early summer he had five thousand men—one quarter of the entire U.S. Army—in the field. Adding their numbers to the roughly three thousand Mexican soldiers scouring

Chihuahua and Sonora, the several hundred Indian scouts still in service, and the numerous bands of vaqueros and volunteers out hunting Apaches, one arrives at a total of nearly nine thousand armed men pursuing eighteen Chiricahua warriors, thirteen women, and six children.[8]

But they could never catch him. Finally, after months of living on the move, Geronimo surrendered. Having trekked throughout Southeast Arizona where this all took place, I am amazed at his ability to be so elusive. What made it so difficult was that the American army employed traditional strategic thinking. The same kind used in the Civil War where armies lined up in neat and tidy lines across from one another and advanced on each other. The Apache utilized guerrilla warfare tactics. Hit and run. Hit and run. Stick to the mountains while the army followed waterways. It wasn't until General Crook began using Apache scouts

---

[8] Roberts, *Once They Moved Like the Wind*, 283.

from different bands that they made any headway.

The questions for us today would be along the lines of asking what divergent thinking looks like in ministry, missionary, and church planting circles. Knowing that ultimately "nothing is new under the sun" what innovations and fusions are swelling the ground beneath us like a coming earthquake? More than being trendy ... what font to use in graphic design or the latest worship music trends ... what innovations are before us or beneath us? How would we know? Is it like skinny jeans in that as soon as you catch up, the trend or wave has already moved on? Possibly.

Who's the misfit among the people you know? Who employs divergent thinking that you could glean from? How do you cultivate such outside-the-box innovations in your life? How will you be exposed to new and different ideas that are light years ahead of anything you'll sit through at the next Exponential Conference?

Misfits are visionaries. They come up with different solutions to issues or problems at hand. They ask questions. At times, uncomfortable questions. We desperately need to hear their voices.

We need more misfits in North American church planting today. Settlers, institutions, and established voices rule the day. Solutions to problems end up simply reinforcing and expanding what's already in place. As a result, we tweak assessments, set planters up with coaches, and alter delivery methods for training purposes. More money is thrown at church planting as a whole. But what does not get discussed is whether these solutions are even pertinent and relevant.

In many ways, we're coming up with answers for questions that are not even being asked. That's because we're asking the wrong kinds of questions. We've so professionalized church planting and made it a lucrative industry that we continue to keep doing much of it the same, but with better videos, better social media, more material, more training, more conferences, and the like. The cycle continues and we wonder why we don't see any semblance of a church planting movement. In the midst of this, I continue to ask why all of the trendy, hip, and cool places receive all of the church planters whereas neighborhoods, cities, towns, and villages on the decline, that are struggling and being written off as unimportant, receive little to no church planters? Such questions get drowned out in the hype known as church planting.

We need more misfits.

Although they are misunderstood and marginalized, they are gifts to the church. They think differently. We need that more than ever before. We need the equivalent of Martin Luther's *Ninety-five Theses* which he nailed to the door of the church at Wittenberg more than 500 years ago. We need people who will go against the grain not out of angst, but out of a burning realization that we need something new. Something better. And they have a new idea of what's needed.

Who knows? Maybe the coronavirus pandemic was the unintentional disruptor we needed for the local church. Time will tell.

Through Barren Wastelands

CHAPTER 7

Running to the Blank Spaces on the Map

Life is a lot like various video games I've seen over the years. Usually the hero or main character begins at one spot on the map. When you click on "map view" it only shows the tiny portion of what the character has already seen. Everything else? Black. Blank. Beyond the boundaries of experience. Unknown.

We all start life like that. We know what we know. Where we are and no further. Tiny points on the global map. Obviously, the more we travel and experience, the more we see. Our maps enlarge. I'm not as much concerned about whether you've traveled the world over as that is more often the result of privilege or opportunity than anything else. I see this in my classroom every week. Students are pining for travel and experiences. *Most* don't come from backgrounds of means or privilege. In their words (as we just talked about in class) they're "broke college students."

But lacking means or privilege doesn't mean we're relegated to a mundane, boring life without any sense of challenge, purpose, or adventure. On the contrary, we grow complacent about what is right outside our door. We are surrounded by enormous blank swaths on our personal map. Not all adventures need to be far off to be meaningful. They could happen within the city, in rural hinterlands, or in wilderness areas.

A few weeks ago, my oldest son Grant took one such adventure. After a mere eighty-minute drive, he was camping high up on the back side of Mt Hood next to a small river. With panoramic views of the surrounding valleys and at times glimpses of the glaciated volcanic peak itself, it is surprising how in the time it takes to watch a movie one can be deep into the wilderness. Sometimes I need to remind myself of how spectacular is the place where I live.

Even closer yet, over this past weekend, I went to a football game with two of my sons at the nearby Lewis and Clark College. While I've been there numerous times for games I had yet to explore the campus. At halftime we decided, with cameras in hand, to check it out. It was like stepping into a whole new and previously hidden world. We quickly forgot about the game as we wandered, took photos, and talked. I was surprised as to how fun that simple little adventure was. According to Google Maps, it was only six miles from home. But it was as new and exciting as camping on Mt Hood. Sure enough we made our way back to the game mid-third quarter. They won.

I am compelled by blank spaces on the map. My map. My map is different than yours. I've always been motivated by living farther and farther out from where I started my journey in small-town Iowa. I recall when we first moved to the Pacific Northwest, it was almost a compulsion. *I must. I can't live unless I at least try. I don't even care if I fail.* So, with a lot of risk, much uncertainty, and fear, we moved. It hasn't been easy by any stretch but it has been life-changing. There truly has been a lot of failure dotted throughout our decade here. I also understand for those who grew up here that there is a sense of mundaneness and boredom. Their map is different than mine.

This is about more than geography. It can apply as well to our lives and ministries. I've personally started various ventures simply to see and experience what it was all about. From churches to a publishing company to a coffee roasting company to ministries and more. Each time I was stepping into what was previously blank on my map. I didn't *know* until I *knew.*

Maps are also changing. In this case I'm speaking in terms of the front edge of missions or ministry engagement. Like a scene out of an otherworldly science fiction movie, the whole landscape continues to shift and contort. Seemingly every few years or decades, the landscape before us goes through a massive metamorphosis. It is quite disorienting.

It's like as soon as we figure out our map and what surrounds us, those familiar contours shift. It's maddening. It took years into this current metamorphosis for me to see what was going on. I was so disoriented I thought I was literally experiencing a mental health crisis. I had lost my love for the city, particularly the urban core. I had dropped out of my PhD program in urban studies just as I was diving deep into such disciplines as urban planning, transportation planning, and community development. But what drew me there in the first place?

The map. *My* map.

Nearly twenty years ago in the world of church planting, the urban cores of cities were neglected, overlooked, and passed over in favor of the suburbs. Most new churches were suburban. However, the side story and the data suggest this was on par with population growth and dispersion. Meaning, roughly seventy percent of the population of a metro area lies not in the central city but in the suburbs. If you were to overlay a map of where churches were being planted, it shouldn't be shocking that roughly seventy percent of all new churches *then* were suburban. That was based on research conducted between 2000 and 2009.

But the map shifted. Contorted. Transformed right before our eyes.

The scales have tipped inexorably towards planting churches not simply in the city, but especially in the urban core. What was once a new frontier and a blank spot on the map for many denominations and church planting networks now has become mapped and settled. In case you're wondering, a hundred years ago it once was previously mapped and explored. There is an enormous supply of church buildings from that era that can attest to this. Unfortunately, simultaneously with White Flight in the mid-1900s, many churches either moved to the suburbs or disbanded completely.

Fast forward a couple of decades and the narrative has shifted. Church planting in the city, running on parallel tracks of gentrification, has meant that for white folks who had left the city, *their* new frontier is the city. However, we know that throughout all of these transitions, the black church never left the city which they had already mapped and explored throughout the twentieth century.

Now the landscape has shifted again. White church planters are moving en masse to the city center and black churches are selling their buildings (or renting them out) to white churches and following their people to the suburbs. So what does this mean for our maps? That they are ever-changing and rarely static.

That's why I've shifted my focus to the places on the map that no one really wants to go to. These could be particular neighborhoods in a metro area. Or small towns that have been forgotten, neglected, and overlooked, especially in light of this massive mission shift towards urban centers.

If there's ever a continuous yet ever-changing frontier for missions in North America, it is this—the forgotten places. These are places not viewed as or deemed livable or full of people who'll never make the Top 10 list of people that need new churches. More than likely it's because they represent forgotten, marginalized, and lower-income communities. They're not "Instagram-worthy." Since church planters are all too often focused on building their own brands and platforms than to go among the marginalized and outcasts, that does not bode well for these communities. That's why there are countless numbers of churches being started among white hipsters living in the city.

The good news about this new frontier, while it is ever-changing, is that it is right before our eyes. We don't have to even leave our cities or regions. At times they can represent populations that are "less reached" than foreign countries where we continue to send mission workers. That is the challenge before us when we think and talk about North America as a mission field (which it is). It's not as glamorous and exotic as some distant land among people who speak a different tongue. It's not as awe-inspiring as the stories missionaries tell when back in the States on furlough. It doesn't quite make for appealing stories in the regular missionary newsletters. Why? Because we're talking about *our* home *here*. Our cities, towns, states, and regions.

These blank spots are all around us. Even within Portland, a hotbed for church planting, I can point to many places around the metro area that planters mysteriously seem to avoid. I can also point to the same central city neighborhoods where there are so many church planters that their congregations are all meeting on Sundays mere blocks from one another.

It is time to see our home cities, home regions, and home states as mission fields. Even though that probably goes against everything you've been taught in church concerning the false dichotomy we created of *there* versus *here*. Unless we correct our thinking, we'll continue to overlook and forego the blank spaces on the map in favor of what's alluring and cool.

That's why we need explorers, pioneers, and misfits. We desperately need those intrepid souls to keep exploring new terrain, establishing a presence, as well as calling on the church to creatively find new ways to be the church (i.e., the called-out, sent ones) in a truly contextualized manner. This is certainly not for the faint of heart.

I was reminded of this last night.

In one of our Intrepid cohorts, we were talking about the role of pioneers or innovators on the continuum of movements. There are always those who go ahead and forge new paths. However, while we celebrate them, there is also the realization that those who do so risk being misunderstood, alone, and embarking with almost no map available. Each and every person in the cohort admitted to feeling regularly misunderstood, especially in light of launching social enterprises as part of their church planting strategy. They're constantly having to explain to donors and supporting churches what they're doing and why.

The great irony of this whole conversation is that it is really about geography. Meaning, if these church planters and entrepreneurs did this identical work somewhere *over there* (i.e., in a foreign land) then they'd be applauded, encouraged, and held up as innovative. However, on our home turf they're viewed as a bit odd since church planting is to be done a "certain way" *here* versus *there*. Geography.

That's why I've called this book *Through Barren Wastelands*. It's not as much about specific geographic settings (although it certainly is) but because sometimes the wastelands represent isolation and feelings of aloneness. It is tough. Very tough. It is a lonely stretch of open road.

If you've never travelled along these remote highways, you're missing out. Usually they're found in places like Nevada, California, and Arizona. You'll drive for endless miles without seeing anything but desert. Wilderness. Barrenness. Ironically though, these places feed my soul. I need open spaces. I've finally grown comfortable with silence, obscurity, and being alone. The less I track the church planting world online and via social media the more my soul is set free. All of those nagging voices of "should" and "ought" are muffled and forgotten.

I am free. You are free. Sure, this is a lonely road. No, I'm not talking about isolating from friends, family, and colleagues. I'm talking about being content with being misunderstood, forgotten, overlooked, and sidelined as "interesting." But I have a feeling that if you're truly an explorer, pioneer, or a misfit, it doesn't matter anyway. You've grown comfortable in your own skin. Your internal GPS, guided by the Holy Spirit, is all you need as you eschew the crowd and noise to go and do what you truly feel God is leading you to do.

Grab that wheel ... those handlebars ... and take comfort knowing you're who God made you to be and doing the kind of work he has called you to. Build a trail. Start a business. Plant a church.

Bibliography

Batterson, Mark. *Wild Goose Chase: Reclaim the Adventure of Pursuing God*. Colorado Springs: Multnomah, 2008.

Mann, Charles C. *1491: New Revelations of the Americas Before Columbus*. New York: Vintage, 2006.

Roberts, David. *Once They Moved Like the Wind: Cochise, Geronimo, and the Apache Wars*. New York: Touchstone, 1994.

Schuurman, Douglas. J. *Vocation: Discerning Our Callings in Life*. Grand Rapids: Wm. B. Eerdmans, 2004.

Udall, Stewart L. *Majestic Journey: Coronado's Inland Empire*. Santa Fe: Museum of New Mexico Press, 1995.

About the Author

Sean Benesh lives in Portland, Oregon leading Intrepid and teaching at two local universities.

www.seanbenesh.com
@seanbenesh

Made in the USA
Monee, IL
30 October 2023

45456303R00089